LIFE CYCLES

RAINFOREST

Sean Callery

Consultant: David Burnie

KINGFISHER

NEW YORK

KINGFISHER
LONDON & NEW YORK

Distributed in the U.S. by Macmillan,
175 Fifth Ave., New York, NY 10010

Library of Congress Cataloging-in-Publication data has been applied for.

ISBN 978-0-7534-6576-9

Kingfisher books are available for special promotions and premiums.
For details contact: Special Markets Department, Macmillan,
175 Fifth Ave., New York, NY 10010.

For more information, please visit www.kingfisherbooks.com

Printed in China
1 3 5 7 9 8 6 4 2
1TR/0311/WKT/UNTD/140MA

Note to readers: the website addresses listed in this book are correct at
the time of going to print. However, due to the ever-changing nature
of the Internet, website addresses and content can change. Websites
can contain links that are unsuitable for children. The publisher cannot
be held responsible for changes in website addresses or content, or for
information obtained through a third party. We strongly advise that
Internet searches should be supervised by an adult.

The publisher would like to thank the following for permission to reproduce their material. Every care has been taken to trace copyright holders. However, if there have
been unintentional omissions or failure to trace copyright holders, we apologize and will, if informed, endeavor to make corrections in any future edition.
top = t; bottom = b; center = c; left = l; right = r

All artwork Stuart Jackson-Carter (Peter Kavanagh Art Agency)

Cover Shutterstock/Eduardo Rivero; pages 2 Shutterstock/Dr. Morley Read; 3 Shutterstock/Le Do; 4tr Shutterstock/Dr. Morley Read; 4bl Photolibrary/Imagebroker.net; 4br
Alamy/Jacques Jangoux; 5tl Alamy/Chris Mattison; 5tr Photolibrary/All Canada Photos; 5bl Shutterstock/Lim Yong Hian; 5br Naturepl/Pete Oxford; 6bl Alamy/
Redmond Durrell; 6tr Frank Lane Picture Agency (FLPA)/Mark Moffett/Minden; 6br Alex Wild Insects; 7tl Shutterstock/Dr. Morley Read; 7tr Alamy/Alex Bramwell;
7ctr Shutterstock/Dr. Morley Read; 7cr Alex Wild Insects; 7cbr FLPA/Mark Moffett/Minden; 7br Shutterstock/camellia; 8bl Photolibrary/imagebroker.net; 8tr FLPA/
L. Lee Rue; 8br Getty/NGS; 9tl FLPA/Claus Meyer/Minden; 9bl Getty/NGS; 9tr Shutterstock/Madien; 9ctr FLPA/Nobert Wu/Minden; 9cr Alamy/Rolf Nussbaumer;
9cbr Photolibrary/imagebroker.net; 9br Shutterstock/Lim Yong Hian; 10tl Shutterstock; 10tr FLPA/Foto Natura/Minden; 10br Photolibrary/Peter Arnold Images; 11tl
Naturepl/Pete Oxford; 11bl Photolibrary/Wendy Shatil; 11tr Shutterstock/LilKar; 11ctr Shutterstock/worlswildlifewonders; 11cr Naturepl/Pete Oxford; 11cbr Specialist
Stock; 11bcr Shutterstock/Andrejs Pidjass; 11br Shutterstock/ecoventurestravel; 12bl Alamy/Louise Heusinkveld; 12tr Lyn Finn; 12br Robert Whyte/SaveOurWaterNow;
13tl Shutterstock/C. L. Chang; 13bl Robert Whyte/SaveOurWaterNow; 13tr Shutterstock/Lim Yong Hian; 13ctr Corbis/Darrell Gulin/Science Faction; 13cr Science Photo
Library/Eye of Science; 13bcr Lyn Finn; 13br Shutterstock/Lim Yong Hian; 14bl Naturepl/Nick Garbutt; 15tl Alamy/Chris Mattison; 15tr Shutterstock/Ultrashock; 15ctr
Getty/Minden; 15cr FLPA/Dembinsky Photo Assoc.; 15cbr Alamy/Chris Mattison; 15br Shutterstock/Sakir N.; 16bl FLPA/Frans Lanting; 17tr Shutterstock/Sergey Skiezneev;
17ctr Getty/NGS; 17cr FLPA/Frans Lanting; 17cbr FLPA/Frans Lanting; 17br Shutterstock/optimarc; 18bl Naturepl/Tony Heald; 18tr Photoshot/NHPA/ANT; 18br
Photolibrary/Kelvin Aitken; 19tl Photolibrary/Peter Arnold Images; 19bl Auscape/Frank Woerle; 19tr Shutterstock/Lim Yong Hian; 19ctr Shutterstock/Andriy Markov; 19cr
Shutterstock/voylodyon; 19cbr Shutterstock/siart; 19br Alamy/Arco Images GmbH; 20bl FLPA/Thomas Marent; 20br Photolibrary/Garden Picture Library; 21tl Alamy/Kjell
Sandved; 21tr Shutterstock/Wong Yu Liang; 21ctr Shutterstock/Liew Wenf Keong; 21cr FLPA/David Hosking; 21cbr FLPA/Michael Jrabs/Imagebroker; 21br
Shutterstock/Adisa; 22bl FLPA/Piotr Nasrecki; 22tr Nick Garbutt/Indri Images; 23tl Photolibrary/age footstock; 23tr Shutterstock/sydeen; 23ctr FLPA/Piotr Nasrecki; 23cr
Alamy/Christ Mattison; 23cbr FLPA/Chris Mattison; 23br Shutterstock/Lim Yong Hian; 24bl Naturepl/Nick Garbutt; 24tr Naturepl/Nick Garbutt; 24br FLPA/Kevin
Schafer/Minden; 25tl Naturepl/Nick Garbutt; 25bl Naturepl/Nick Garbutt; 25tr Shutterstock/kaarsten; 25ctr FLPA/Kevin Schafer/Minden; 25cr Naturepl/Nick Garbutt; 25cbr
Photoshot/NHPA; 25br Shutterstock/Le Do; 26bl FLPA/David Hosking; 26br Rod Foster/ pyhtonsandboas.co.uk; 27tl Naturepl/Edwin Giesbers; 27tr
Shutterstock/juliengrondin; 27ctr Naturepl/Inaki Relanzon; 27cr Alamy/National Geographic Image Collection; 27br Alamy/All Canada Photos; 27br Shutterstock/encikat;
30tl Shutterstock/David Davis; 30tr Shutterstock/Vaclav Volrab; 30bl Shutterstock/Ambient ideas; 30br Shutterstock/guentermanaus; 31tr Shutterstock/Yu Lan; 31cr
Shutterstock/ClimberJAK; 31br Shutterstock/C. L. Chang; 32tl Shutterstock/wcpmedia; 32br Shutterstock/Dirk Ercken

Contents

Introduction

Rainforests are thick forests where it is warm and wet all year round. These are the perfect conditions for life, and half of all the world's animals live here.

All animals must eat to survive. Their lives are a deadly game of hide-and-seek as they look for food and try to avoid predators. The list of who eats who is called a food chain.

Insects such as this beetle are called consumers because they survive by eating other living things. They usually eat plants, and larger animals eat them.

NORTH AMERICA

rainforests of Central America

Amazon rainforest

equator

SOUTH AMERICA

Plants such as this orchid are at the start of most food chains. They are called producers because they make their own food from the energy of the Sun.

Animals such as tree frogs can be next in the chain. They are consumers, too, catching and eating smaller, slower animals and insects. They are, in turn, eaten by bigger, faster predators.

This book takes you through three food chains from rainforests in different parts of the world. You will learn about the life cycles of ten animals and one plant: how they are born, grow, reproduce, and die.

EUROPE

ASIA

AFRICA

Congo River basin rainforest

Borneo rainforests

Madagascar rainforests

AUSTRALIA

At the top of a food chain is a predator such as this harrier hawk, which is so big, strong, and fast that no other animal can catch it.

Leafcutter ant

Leafcutter ants are farmers in the Amazon rainforest. They collect pieces of leaves and carry them to their nest—not to eat, but to chew into a squishy pulp. They eat the fungus that grows on the pulp.

1 The queen ant mates with smaller male ants as she flies. Then her wings fall off and she digs a nest and lays her eggs.

2 After 7–14 days, the eggs hatch into larvae. They look like worms and have no eyes or legs. As they grow, they shed their skin many times.

4 After a month, the ants emerge as adults. The queen produces eggs throughout her life, and the ant colony keeps growing, with each generation of worker ants taking care of the one that comes next.

3 The larvae start to grow legs and eyes. They are now called pupae.

Did you know?

Leafcutter ants may carry pieces of leaves 820 feet (250m) back to the nest. They can carry 30 times their own weight.

The ants have scissorlike mouths, called mandibles, to cut up leaves.

Other ants in the colony fight off attackers if they try to raid the nest.

Most ants live only for about six months, but queen ants can stay alive for 14 years unless something sniffs them out . . .

Armadillo

Armadillos sniff out ants and termites with their long noses. They dig into the nests with their sharp claws and scoop up the insects on their sticky tongues.

1 Nine-banded armadillos usually live alone in underground burrows, but they meet up to mate.

2 After four months, the mother gives birth to four babies. These are identical because they have grown from the same egg. Their skin is very soft.

4 In six months, the young are ready to leave. Adult armadillos are good swimmers. Their shells are heavy, so they gulp in a lot of air to help them stay afloat.

3 Armadillo babies feed on their mother's milk for three months. The skin on their backs hardens to form a tough shell within weeks.

Did you know?

An armadillo's shell is made from overlapping bands of special bone, with skin in between so it can bend.

If it is frightened, the nine-banded armadillo jumps in the air and then sprints away.

An armadillo's two front claws are especially long and sharp, which makes them excellent for digging.

Nine-banded armadillos can live for more than ten years unless something finds a way through their armor . . .

Jaguar

The jaguar is one of the biggest, strongest hunters in the rainforest. It eats any animal it can kill, including armadillos, monkeys, deer, birds, and snakes. It swims well, so it eats fish, too.

1 Jaguars live alone and meet only to mate. After 13 weeks, the female gives birth to between two and four cubs.

2 Jaguar cubs are blind for the first two weeks of life. They feed on their mother's milk for three months and stay in the den with her until they are six months old.

Did you know?

A jaguar's fur is covered with rosette-shaped spots that help it hide among the shadows on the forest floor.

Jaguars kill their prey by biting through its skull with their powerful jaws.

A jaguar's claws are sharp, curved, and good for holding on to prey and climbing. The claws pull in when they are not needed.

4 Adult jaguars can run fast only for short distances. They do not chase their prey but creep up on it from behind.

3 The cubs hunt with their mother for up to two years and practice their hunting skills by play fighting. Then they leave to find their own territory.

Jaguars are at the top of their food chain. They can live for 15 years. The only threat to their survival is humans.

Bluebottle butterfly

Butterflies perform a magical dance through the rainforests of Borneo as their brightly colored wings flutter from flower to flower. A butterfly's life cycle is full of dramatic changes.

1 After mating, the female butterfly lays tiny eggs on the young leaves of plants, sticking them down with a special glue.

2 Within a week, a gray caterpillar hatches from each egg. It soon turns green to blend in with the leaves. It eats and eats until it is fat and about 1 inch (3cm) long.

4 During three weeks inside the chrysalis, the pupa changes into a butterfly. This is called metamorphosis. The butterfly emerges from the chrysalis and flies away.

3 The caterpillar is fully grown after four weeks. It spins itself a case called a chrysalis out of silk thread. It is now called a pupa.

Did you know?

Butterflies use their hollow tongues to suck up nectar from flowers and the juice of rotting fruit.

Butterfly wings are covered with thousands of tiny, colorful, overlapping scales.

Bluebottle butterfly caterpillars scare off predators by growing two yellow horns on their heads. The horns smell bad.

Butterflies such as this one can live for several months. But there is something in the rainforest that can trap them . . .

Pitcher plant

Pitcher plants eat animals. Insects and even larger creatures become trapped in their jug-shaped pots and are digested in the juices at the bottom.

1 A seed germinates and grows into a small leafy plant. It can take a whole year to grow just 1 inch (2.5cm). Each leaf produces a long, thin stem called a tendril.

2 The tendrils develop leafy flaps that curve and grow bigger at the end, forming small jugs. These are the pitchers.

4 The plant flowers, and each tiny flower releases up to 500 feather-light seeds that are carried away on the wind. Many seeds are eaten by animals, but a few land on the soil and grow into new plants.

3 Sweet-smelling nectar attracts insects, which slip down inside the pitchers, fall into the juices at the bottom, and drown. The plant digests their bodies.

Did you know?

Pitcher plants are sometimes called "monkey cups" because monkeys drink the liquid trapped in the pots.

Large beetles and even animals as big as rats can slip down the pitcher's sticky walls. There is no escape!

Each pot has a lid that stops rain from thinning the liquid at the bottom. It also smells like nectar, which attracts insects.

Pitcher plants live for many years, but the jugs can be badly damaged by animals looking for food inside . . .

Western tarsier

Tarsiers look like teddy bears wearing sunglasses, but they are not cuddly! These primates eat living animals and are sometimes attracted to dying ones trapped inside pitcher plants.

1 Western tarsiers give birth to only one baby at a time. A newborn tarsier has fur and can open its eyes.

2 Sometimes the mother carries the baby around, but more often she leaves it on a branch when she goes off to hunt.

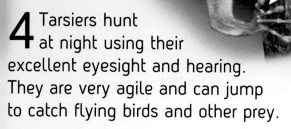

4 Tarsiers hunt at night using their excellent eyesight and hearing. They are very agile and can jump to catch flying birds and other prey.

3 Young tarsiers learn how to hunt while they are still being fed their mother's milk.

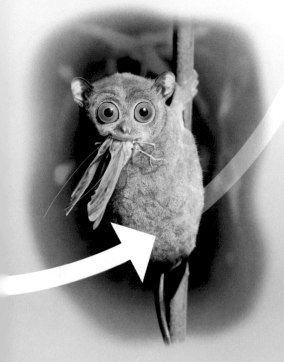

Did you know?

When attacked by a predator, a tarsier opens its eyes very wide and shows its teeth.

A tarsier's large ears help it hear insects, birds, lizards, bats, and snakes moving in the darkness.

Tarsiers have pads like suction cups on the ends of their fingers and toes to help them grip smooth tree bark.

Tarsiers live for about 12 years. At times, they go down to the ground for water. Sometimes an animal snaps them up . . .

Saltwater crocodile

Saltwater crocodiles live in any type of water—from oceans to the rivers and pools in the rainforest. They lurk, ready to leap up and grab prey in their strong jaws.

1 The female lays 60–80 eggs. She guards the nest well to protect the eggs from predators.

2 After 80 days, the babies use a special tooth to break a hole in their shells. They call out to their mother, and sometimes she helps them hatch.

4 When they have learned to hunt, the young crocodiles are ready to find their own territory. No prey is too large for an adult, on land or in the water.

3 The mother carries the hatchlings to the water. She protects and feeds them for eight weeks while they learn to swim.

Did you know?

Crocodile teeth are hollow. New teeth grow inside the old ones, so if a tooth falls out, a new one takes its place.

With their eyes on top of their heads, crocodiles are able to watch for prey while they lie hidden in the water.

A crocodile's powerful tail is useful for swimming and for attacking: one blow is enough to break a victim's legs.

Saltwater crocodiles are a top predator because no other animal is able to kill them. They can live for 50–75 years.

Giraffe weevil

Giraffe weevils are beetles that have long, thin, giraffelike necks. They live in the rainforests on the island of Madagascar and feed on plants, seeds, and leaves.

1 The female weevil rolls a leaf around her head and neck to make a tube. Then she lays her eggs inside the tube.

2 A larva hatches from each egg and starts to eat the leaf. Every so often it sheds its outer skeleton as it grows.

4 The pupa metamorphoses into an adult weevil with wings and legs and emerges from the cocoon.

3 The larva eats more of the leaf, which turns brown. Inside the leaf tube, the larva spins a silk cocoon around itself and changes into a pupa. The leaf and pupa drop to the ground.

Did you know?

The male giraffe weevil has a longer neck than the female. A long neck makes the male more attractive as a mate.

Like other insects, the giraffe weevil has its skeleton on the outside. It is made of hard plates like a suit of armor.

The beetles use their antennae for smelling food, finding a mate, and sensing movements that could spell danger.

Some weevils live for days; others live for years. They fight off small predators, but sticky tongues mean big trouble . . .

21

Tree frog

Tree frogs climb and jump among the branches and hop down to the forest floor. They flick out their long, sticky tongues to catch insects along the way.

1 The female leaves her tree, finds a stream, and lays 200 eggs on overhanging plants. The eggs are stuck together in jelly so that they cannot be washed away.

2 Tadpoles grow inside the eggs, and when they are strong enough, they break free. They are like tiny fish that flick their tails to swim. They breathe through gills.

Did you know?

Tree frogs jump and land safely because they have special sticky pads on their fingers and toes.

Unlike many other frogs, a tree frog's eyes face the front so that they can judge distances for jumping.

All frogs breathe through their skin, which is moist and as thin as paper.

4 After about 16 weeks, the young frogs are ready to leave the water and find a tree to live in. They do not return to the water until it is time for them to breed.

3 The tadpoles grow legs. They develop lungs so that they can breathe air, and their tails disappear, too.

Some tree frogs live for only a year. Others live longer if they can stay away from beady eyes and busy beaks . . .

Helmet vanga

The helmet vanga lives deep in the rainforest. It sits on a tree's lower branches, from where it can easily swoop down on its prey.

1 A pair of birds builds a cup-shaped nest from twigs, roots, and leaves. They balance it where tree branches make a fork shape.

2 The female lays up to three eggs. Sometimes other vangas help the parents by sitting on the eggs to keep them warm.

4 Helmet vangas sit still in trees. They are usually hard to see until they fly out suddenly and snatch prey on the ground.

3 When the chicks hatch, one parent keeps guard while the other hunts for food. The chicks' dull plumage helps keep them well hidden from predators.

A helmet vanga has a large, curved beak for holding and crunching up prey.

Adult vangas feed snails, lizards, spiders, crabs, and frogs to their chicks.

A helmet vanga has short wings and a stocky body, so it cannot fly far.

No one is sure how long helmet vangas live. It depends on whether they can keep away from sneaky predators . . .

Tree boa

The tree boa hides among the branches or on the forest floor, ready to pounce on victims such as birds, lizards, and rodents.

1 While some snakes lay eggs, boas give birth to live young. Six months after mating, a female tree boa has between four and 15 babies.

2 The juvenile boas keep the bright red color they had when they were born. It might help scare off predators by making the young snakes look poisonous.

4 Adult boas lie still and wait for their prey. When it comes close, they grab it with their teeth, coil their body around it, and squeeze until it stops breathing.

3 The young snakes are 16 inches (40cm) long. They shed their skin as they grow and begin to turn brown or gray-green. It takes more than one year for them to become adults.

Did you know?

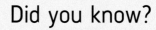

 Snakes smell with their tongues. They flick them all the time to sense what is on the ground and in the air.

 Snakes cannot blink. Their eyes are covered by clear eyelids, so they stay open even when a snake sleeps.

 Boas can open their mouths very wide to swallow their meals whole.

Boas live up to 30 years. Once they are adults, very few animals are able to attack them.

An Amazon food web

This book follows three rainforest food chains. Most animals eat more than one food, however, so they are part of several food chains. There are many food chains in a single rainforest, and they link like a map to make a food web.

jaguar

rodent

monkey

eagle

armadillo

snake

parrot

spider

insect

flowers

amphibian

leaves

ant

reptile

fruit

This is a food web from the Amazon rainforest.

Glossary

AGILE
Being able to move quickly and easily.

BURROW
A hole or tunnel in the ground, used as shelter by an animal.

CAMOUFLAGE
Blending in with the surroundings to avoid being seen easily.

CHRYSALIS
A hard outer case made by a butterfly or moth when it is changing shape.

COLONY
A group of insects, animals, or plants of the same type that live close together.

CONSUMER
A living thing that survives by eating other living things.

DIGEST
When the body breaks down food to get the nutrients, or goodness, that will keep it alive.

FUNGUS
A living thing that absorbs food from living or dead things around it.

GERMINATE
When a seed first starts to grow and release shoots.

GILLS
The organs used to breathe underwater.

HATCHLING
An animal just born from a hard-shelled egg.

IDENTICAL
Looking the same.

JUVENILE
Another word for young.

LARVA
A young insect that will change its body shape to become an adult. Groups are called larvae.

MANDIBLE
The biting mouthpart of an insect.

METAMORPHOSIS
When a young insect changes its body shape in stages on the way to becoming an adult.

NECTAR
The sweet liquid made by flowers to attract insects, birds, and other animals.

PLUMAGE
A bird's feathers.

PREDATOR
An animal that kills and eats other animals.

PREY
An animal that is hunted by a predator.

PRIMATE
A mammal with flexible fingers and toes, and eyes that face forward.

PRODUCER
A living thing that makes its own food from the energy of the Sun.

PUPA
The stage when a young insect rests before changing its body shape.

REPRODUCTION
The way that insects, animals, and plants have babies.

RODENT
A gnawing animal, such as a mouse or a rat.

SKELETON
The set of bones inside a living thing's body. Insects have their skeletons on the outside.

TADPOLE
The form of a frog before it is an adult.

TENDRIL
A long, thin part of a climbing plant.

TERMITE
An insect that feeds on wood, leaves, and soil.

TERRITORY
The area where an animal hunts and keeps out rivals.

These websites have information about rainforests or their animals—or both!

- bbc.co.uk/cbbc/wild/amazon
- enchantedlearning.com/subjects/rainforest
- factzoo.com
- globio.org/glossopedia/Default.aspx
  (then search for "rainforest")
- kids.mongabay.com/elementary/201.html
- kids.nationalgeographic.com/kids/animals/
  creaturefeature

31

Index